IN THE COMPANY OF QUEENS

poems by

Carol Milkuhn

Finishing Line Press
Georgetown, Kentucky

IN THE COMPANY
OF QUEENS

ACKNOWLEDGMENTS

Anne Boleyn's Dressmaker: Winner of Marian Gleason Award, published in
2001 edition of *The Mountain Troubadour* and in the 2008 edition of *Vermont
Literary Review*. Second Place winner in 2012 Persona Contest sponsored by
Maine Poets Society. Published online in *The Copperfield Review*, Winter, 2014.

Jane Seymour's Gardener: Winner of the Goldstein Memorial Award. Published
in the 2013 edition of *The Mountain Troubadour*.

Katherine Howard's Portrait Painter: Published in the 2005 edition of *The
Mountain Troubadour*. Published online in *The Copperfield Review*, Winter 2014.

The Rough Wooing: Winner of Most Highly Commended Award in the 2012
Margaret Reid Contest sponsored by Winning Writers. Published online at the
Winning Writers website.

Publisher: Leah Maines

Editor: Christen Kincaid

Cover Art: Judy Brook

Author Photo: Judy Brook

Cover Design: Elizabeth Maines

Printed in the USA on acid-free paper.
Order online: www.finishinglinepress.com
also available on amazon.com

Author inquiries and mail orders:
Finishing Line Press
P. O. Box 1626
Georgetown, Kentucky 40324
U. S. A.

Table of Contents

For Armando Henriquez, friend and mentor, in memory.

*And for my Burlington Poetry Group—Judy Brook,
Alice Christian, Nancy Gilbert, Sue London, Inga Potter,
and Nancy Richardson—
with appreciation for their help and support.*

Retirement brings the gift of time, time I have spent pursuing my dream of being a writer. And, since I have long been fascinated by the queens of Britain, I turned to this subject when I picked up a pen, exploring my interest through both prose and poetry.

In the Company of Queens tells the stories of many queens, including all six of Henry VIII's wives. One of the poems in this cycle, "Anne Boleyn's Dressmaker," was especially pivotal for me; in time this needlewoman would acquire a name, a husband, and a career, evolving into the main character in my novel, *A Tapestry of Queens*.

Over the years I have continued to interweave the strands of poetry and prose. In "The Rough Wooing," I pick up the story of Marie de Guise, a queen I first wrote about in *A Tapestry of Queens*. But, unlike the novel, Marie de Guise's story does not end in 1542; "The Rough Wooing," a narrative poem focusing on Scotland from 1543 to 1548, explores Marie de Guise's success in defending Scotland from the predatory Tudors.

In the Company of Queens also explores the lives and careers of Twentieth Century royals, lives that parallel those of their forebears in surprising ways. But then, in writing about Queen Elizabeth II, Princess Diana, and Kate Middleton, I am writing about women of character and strength—and such women always share characteristics that cross centuries. Such women always inspire.

HOW THE MEDIA SHAPES MONARCHY

Today's headlines focus on several royal events: the birth
of baby George, the wedding of William and Kate,
the Queen's Diamond Jubilee. But Princess Di's
dresses, once front page news, merit only a
mention in *Vanity Fair*. Farther back
the Queen's father overcomes his
stutter just as her uncle marries
Wallis Simpson and then not
much occurs for hundreds
of years to the Victorias,
Georges, and Annes
listed on the
internet
until the Tudors
cross centuries and the
trials and tribulations of the
wives of Henry VIII are found
on Google, followed on Twitter and
featured in *The New York Times.* Anne Boleyn
is romanticized in *Anne of the Thousand Days,* vilified
in *The Other Boleyn Girl* even as the remains of Richard III,
found in a parking lot, become front page news. So present and
past flow freely through this hourglass, Tudors and Windsors slipping
through that narrow neck where of course nothing happened. Not a thing

REFLECTIONS OF CATHERINE OF ARAGON'S SISTER

Crowned Queen of England in 1509, Catherine of Aragon loses her queenly status when she is imprisoned by Henry VIII in 1533. She will die in January, 1536, still confined within the walls of Kimbolton Castle.

When you judge my sister, know
she was once England's queen, wed to one she loved;
her world golden, gladdened by royal pageantry,
by coronations and courtiers, jousts and masques—
a worthy heritage

for as children we laid claim to the Alhambra,
splashed in fountains concealed in secluded cloisters,
watched sunlight dance on Alcazaba's silver cross,
so at home in the Spain our parents had conquered,
so coddled and cosseted

                that she never dreamed
of an unleashed falcon, of naked talons and claws,
of a raven-haired beauty known as Anne Boleyn.
And, if at the end she whispered her husband's name,
forgave his adultery and abandonment,
her heart was unchanging,
as constant as the needle she followed due north
                    to that bleak, wind-swept shore.

ANNE BOLEYN'S DRESSMAKER

Crowned Queen of England in 1533, Anne Boleyn is executed in 1536 on trumped-up charges of adultery.

A dressmaker sees things differently.
Most people remember my lady as wife of a king or mother of a queen,
but I remember that naughty negligee she wore to Henry Tudor's bed—
    black satin drapery I trimmed in orange silk,
    ebony folds flame-frosted, scented with cinnamon and cloves,
    just right for my sophisticated lady,
        who was as feisty and fast-living as the falcon on her crest—
        the kind of woman other women rarely like.

"Raven-haired witch" gossips called her,
citing a blemished fingertip, an extra nail, as proof of Satan's curse.
So I designed a robe with ample sleeves to hide that imperfection—
those jewel-embroidered, fox-lined folds were a secret-smothering sheath.

Still, things fall apart, unravel at the end.
Henry enjoyed a romantic chase, but rarely cared for what he caught.
And my lady knew her worth, wouldn't favor, flatter, or fawn upon a man—
    the kind of woman some women really like.
    I took care she met death as befits a queen, regally arrayed,
    gowned in rose satin offset by gray brocade,
    her feet encased in silver slippers, the cutting edge of fashion,
        filigreed and fragile, never meant for walking.

A DANCE WITH DIANA

Like Anne Boleyn, Princess Di was a fashion plate. Also like her sixteenth century counterpart, Princess Di fascinated wherever she might be—even as she hid the truth of a dysfunctional marriage.

At night she would binge on pints of ice cream

        while accepting John Travolta's outstretched hand,

butterflies in her stomach, satisfying an ache

        she hid under glamorous footage dancing

unforgettably, her velvet gown sweeping

        across the marbled floor of the Reagan White House,

her grievances as a royal captive

        a backdrop momentarily set aside for she was

trapped within a marriage tasting sour and sad,

        seeking sweetness in moments frozen,

                hungry for perfection as a fairytale princess
                moving in harmony with a handsome prince.

JANE SEYMOUR'S GARDENER

Wed to Henry VIII in 1536, just ten days after Anne Boleyn's execution,
Jane Seymour dies in childbirth in 1537.

Just wed, she asked the king for a secret garden,
a place safe from prattling tongues and prying eyes.
So I transformed a far corner of Hampton Court,
designed a refuge for pansies and petunias,
for roses, foxglove and feathery foliage,
        a haven just right for my soft-spoken lady—
        for she had a gentle touch that nurtured all,
        even that rarest bloom: hope in a king's heart.

"Sharp edges are best softened," she frequently vowed,
so I planted heliotrope and hydrangea,
lush cascades of wisteria buzzing with bees,
creating a sanctuary of scents that lured
tiny, weightless wrens and plump, red-breasted robins.
        How she delighted in their high-pitched serenade—
        even as she too blossomed, fertile and fecund,
        pregnant with a royal seed, swollen with a son.

An early, unexpected frost coats all in rime,
covers grasslands and gardens with a platinum shroud,
leaving a staccato brilliance, a sheen behind.
Today my queen will be buried in Westminster,
formally interred beneath blocks of lifeless stone—
        what has she to do with such a dank, dismal nave?
        Best to mourn her in her silvered garden—
        as shining as her soul, too lustrous for the grave.

SURFING WILL AND KATE'S WEBSITE

Here are intricate passageways and blind alleys as impenetrable as Jane Seymour's garden.

It's mostly gossip: a thicket of tittle tattle,
a maze of inviting paths that taper off
into sheltered courtyards hedged by verbiage:
glib descriptions of baby George tottering
in blue-and white overalls and Pre-Walker shoes,
of lace-appliqued wedding dresses, High Street brands,
and of course brunch with the Queen at Buckingham—
a labyrinth, in short, of false starts and dead ends
designed to prevent access to an inner core.
So as I navigate this superficial landscape,
I wonder—if these royals weren't so wary,
so worried about the press and publicity,
would they describe—let's say—
the look in the eyes of a shell-shocked veteran
as he stares uncomprehending, then turns away?

THE ROUGH WOOING

A widowed French noblewoman—and a prize in the royal marriage market—Marie de Guise rejects the marriage proposal of Henry VIII in 1538, saying she has "a slender neck." Instead she marries James V of Scotland; his death in 1542 leaves her widowed a second time—with a week old daughter.

I
Death of a King
Scotland, December 7, 1542

Kneeling on stones in the chapel at Linlithgow,
Marie de Guise heard the creak of an opening door,
and, chilled by a sudden wind, a bitter gust,
ceased praying—even as the flicker of flambeaux
intensified, casting shadows on the floor,
snakes slithering over tombs, writhing in the dust.

Rising, she met the messenger eye-to-eye,
aware his ashen face, deeply creased in agony,
foretold of disaster, of death's reptilian sting.
"I bring you sad news," he said, voice amplified,
echoing, intensifying catastrophe,
"This morning your husband died. Your lord. Our king."

Light-headed with shock, she swayed as she fought for breath;
for she was vulnerable, now widow and mother,
just delivered of a daughter, Scotland's only heir.
Reeling, she replied, "God protects, the Scriptures saith,"
for she knew Scotland was ripe for massacre,
besieged on all sides, with enemies everywhere.

Eyes on the cross, the image of Christ crucified,
she drew a deep breath, praying slowly, silently:
Blessed Mother, as your son was resurrected,
so I know Scotland will be reborn, will survive.
To this end I pledge my life, put my trust in thee,
she vowed, as she crossed herself and genuflected.

II
The Path to War
Scotland, Winter, 1542

As winter's cowl settled over Edinburgh—
a foggy darkness enshrouding one and all —
Scotland's nobles assembled for rites of burial,
formal obsequies befitting a time of woe.
Yet Marie de Guise remained behind Linlithgow's walls—
for she doubted these lairds, deeming most disloyal.

Determined to gain control, the upper hand,
she waited patiently, her daughter at her side,
forcing these treacherous lairds to come to her,
to brave the snow-covered roads of this northern land.
Driven by curiosity, they complied,
bright-eyed, cruelly calculating inquisitors.

Beards frosted white, feet wrapped in ice-encrusted furs,
they circled the cradle, one after another,
like hungry wolves surrounding a potential prey.
For a newborn, nursing infant was their ruler,
her only protection a young, French born mother—
and they were a feckless lot, ready to betray.

Still she won them over. As these lairds sipped rare wines,
warmed bone-chilled hands and feet in front of blazing fires,
they fell under the spell of Marie de Guise—
while she, tireless, pursued her ultimate design:
the crowning of her child—a gesture to inspire
a struggling Scotland, so close to catastrophe.

For, hidden behind the walls of Hampton Court,
England's King Henry, that aging Tudor tyrant,
now a loathsome mass of bloated, quivering flesh,
was greedily glancing north, certain none could thwart
his plan to swallow Scotland whole, to supplant
a weakened Stuart monarchy with a Tudor crest.

III
The Rough Wooing
Edinburgh, winter, 1544

Two winters—a lifetime later—she stood amidst
the smoldering ruins of Holyrood Abbey—
a skeleton whose blackened ribs cried sacrilege,
pled for revenge on the ruthless egotist
who had defiled the tomb where her husband lay,
flanked by their two sons, stones aligned, edge to edge.

A tomb. Sacred soil defiled for a royal bride.
For, spurred on by his insatiable ambition,
King Henry was bent on marriage, pursuing
a union of his only son, his joy and pride,
with her young daughter—a political vision
that had erupted into war—this "rough wooing."

Now, as Marie de Guise surveyed the debris,
she prayed for Scots butchered, skewered on English blades,
their bodies left as carrion along the roadways,
fly-infested, rotting corpses at last retrieved
by shaken survivors of these horrific raids,
souls wounded and lost, scarred by misery and dismay.

As she mourned, sunbeams broke through the cold, granite sky,
highlighting a metal shard in the mangled earth.
Hands trembling, she reached for the consecrated cross,
pulled from the ashes a symbol identified
with a risen Christ, resurrection and rebirth—
a sign the Scots would win, whatever be the cost.

IV

In the Wake of Pinkie Clough
Ichmahome Priory, Scotland, spring, 1548

Gratefully, Marie de Guise awoke to chanting,
soothing notes that lingered, quivered in the air
as the disembodied voices of the brothers
of Ichmahome Priory matched the rising
of the sun, sought the divine in morning prayer—
such blessed music for a troubled mother.

Now, as shafts of sunlight appeared, golden gleams
defining her child's sleeping form, the queen arose,
donned her cloak, and slipped out into a corridor
of filigreed arches framing a square of green.
What can we do? she pondered. *We cannot oppose*
the English; our army is tired, unfit for war.

For early last September, on "Black Saturday,"
Scotland had lost at Pinkie Clough, a rude defeat
that destroyed her fighting forces and, as onerous,
left the unguarded Lowlands under English sway—
a loss that forced Marie de Guise north in retreat
to the Highland wilderness, stark and mountainous.

Now, as she viewed the monks' garden, a place apart,
Marie de Guise took note of opposites:
mint and lady's mantle, aggressive specimens
ruthlessly edging out their fragile counterparts—
delicate flowers so obviously unfit,
so pressed for space in this monastery garden.

Without protection, these flowers will not survive,
she mused, her thoughts turning to her still sleeping child—
then to the message she must answer by eventide.
For the French had offered aid, would her hopes revive—
but her child's home must be in France, not the British Isles,
for her daughter would be *Le Dauphin's* intended bride.

Can I give up my daughter? the queen debated,
entrust her to others, let her be raised elsewhere?
The rich perfume of incense wafted through the air,
sharpening her senses as she deliberated—
without doubt, she must answer the French messenger,
for, with the English close, she had no time to spare.

Pondering, the queen gazed on moors studded with stone,
watched the sun burn through the morning mist, rendering
glen and gulf golden, colored by a molten dawn—
but she knew no joy. Her thoughts on the Scottish throne,
heavy-hearted, she trod the path to its ending—
only to find her chamber empty, her child gone!

Heart hammering against her ribs, the frantic queen
ran through the priory's labyrinthian paths
praying for a glimpse of her daughter's dressing gown,
for telltale movement in a copse of evergreen.
She paused, her breath coming in painful, ragged gasps—
and heard her daughter's laughter—a most blessed sound.

Sitting in a cluster of white-flowering roses,
her hair burnished gold by the dawn's early rays,
Scotland's little queen seemed a delicate fairy—
an elfin child, caught in a moment of repose.
Weak with relief, her mother hugged her runaway—
and made her decision. France was sanctuary.

V
The Tide Turns
Scotland, Fall, 1548

Spared by the English, perched on a rocky hillside,
Stirling Castle was treasured by Marie de Guise—
here was a pleasure palace, a world of opulence,
of lush, terraced gardens, of chambers beautified
by friezes, fretwork, silver-threaded tapestries:
luxuries befitting a royal residence.

But today such elegance left the queen unmoved.
Deep in thought, she sat alone in Stirling's Great Hall
Holding the cross retrieved from Holyrood Abbey—
A twisted piece of metal, soot-encrusted, bruised,
But able to withstand whatever might befall—
This cross inspired her with its resiliency.

Fingering the icon, she prayed for a miracle:
her daughter's safe landing in far-off Brittany.
For storms had vexed the northern waters, creating
crosscurrents punishing, pulsating, powerful—
threatening a child now marked by destiny
to rescue all—by Scotland and France uniting.

Footsteps. A shadow darkening the sunlit floor.
Then booming, joy-filled words from Scotland's Governor—
"Your daughter is safe. Even now she rests at Roscoff."
"Praise God," Marie de Guise replied. "Forevermore,"
she added—as sun brushed the cross, a meteor
picking out silvered streaks beneath the blackened dross.

THE EMBROIDERY INSTRUCTOR OF MARY, QUEEN OF SCOTS

The daughter of Marie de Guise, the little child described in "The Rough Wooing," does marry Le Dauphin of France and is crowned Queen of France. Upon the death of her husband, Mary returns to Scotland, assuming her role as Queen of Scots. In 1568 when a coup d'etat forces her to flee to England, she is imprisoned by her cousin, Elizabeth I of England. In 1587, having spent over twenty years a captive, Mary, Queen of Scots, is beheaded for treason.

I like rubbing against royalty,
thrive on fingering silk and satin, fragile cloth of gold,
delight in awakening a noblewoman's needle.
But I wanted no part of ill-starred Mary Stuart—
I fear women who count their days in cross stitch—women like
     this long widowed, long abandoned,
                   long imprisoned queen.

Yet I was a pawn in a royal game—
so I pretended friendship, praising her as she needled,
taught her to coil colors, secret stitches under strapwork,
enliven a tapestry with panels of birds and beasts,
then dust all with long-stemmed roses, that majesty of red—
innocent pastimes, I thought—tasks to ease the dull days of
     this long widowed, long abandoned,
                   long imprisoned queen.

But a needle can be eloquent.
As I watched, milady embroidered feral creatures:
a fox bursting from brambles, a falcon soaring on high,
even a bear, black-mouthed and bullying—but unfettered and free.
I knew then how this woman suffered—
and if I have held sacred these silk-encrusted linens,
this legacy
     of a long-widowed, long abandoned,
                   long imprisoned queen—
these bits of cloth reflect a captive's life,
           tell of biting anguish,
                of bitterness reborn as art.

LANDMINES

Like Mary, Queen of Scots, Diana, Princess of Wales, lived a tempestuous,
tragic life that ended violently. But Princess Di was no stranger to violence.
After her divorce from Prince Charles in 1996, she toured minefields as
part of her campaign for an international ban on the use of landmines.

Charles' announcement that he had never loved her
blew up the fairy tale underpinning her life,
but he made all so much worse when he told the world—
and their children—that even those sweet beginnings
had been a sham, each of his words an explosive
buried in the warzone of their relationship—
so who can imagine Princess Diana's thoughts
as she walked across that Angolan minefield,
for she knew all about things that, if not defused,
leave us vulnerable, like innocent children
playing with a cache of shrapnel-studded shells.

ANNE OF CLEVES' ACCOUNTANT

The fourth of Henry VIII's six wives, Anne of Cleves catches the King's attention when he sees Holbein's portrait of the German princess. Seeing her in the flesh, however, is a different matter; declaring his new bride "ugly," the King divorces her on July 9, 1540.

At first I discounted King Henry's fourth wife,
dismissed her German accent and drab attire
as insurmountable liabilities—
until I recognized she excelled at math,
knew too well that love was a variable,
an unknown quantity in that equation,
that uneasy imbalance we call marriage.
So I sided with Anne of Cleves, advised her
to divorce her husband, now an aging king
obsessed with his conquest of a young coquette.
And if I am criticized by courtiers
for torching long-cherished institutions,
those sacred ceremonies of yesteryear,
I have no regrets. For—by my addition—
when milady gave up a golden crown
                    she gained things priceless:
her security, freedom, and self-respect.

KATHRYN HOWARD'S PORTRAIT PAINTER

Still in her teens, Kathryn Howard marries the 49 year old King of England on July 28, 1540—just 19 days after divorcing Anne of Cleves. In February, 1542 Kathryn Howard is executed on grounds of adultery.

I meant to paint a masterpiece.
Mine a king's commission, I was perfection-seeking, hard-to-please.
By hand I ground pigment into powder, cinnabar into crimson,
lapis lazuli into ultramarine, washing the canvas
with a rainbow of reds, ruby red, wine red, orange red,
against a background of cerulean blue.
Such a swirl of shades, I thought, would embody royalty,
reflect the beauty of Kathryn Howard, King Henry's beloved queen.

I forgot those shadows that seep to the surface,
                    bleeding through brushwork, destroying design.
Wed to an ailing, aging king,
my lady chose a paramour, risking her crown for a courtier's kiss.
Hers an affair etched in acid, a collage of corroded color
blistered by the red of adultery, that dark and dangerous dye.

For both lady and lover were caught, of course;
then condemned to death, a king's revenge on an adolescent bride.
I left her portrait unsealed and unprotected, despite damp and icy drafts,
watching reds, roughly handled,
                    reduced to russet, purples bruised to plum.
So much beauty wasted.
An old man now, I remember my lady as just sixteen,
her hair a crown uncontained, brushed to a fiery sheen.

REFLECTIONS OF KATHERINE PARR'S JEWELER

The sixth and last wife of Henry VIII, Katherine Parr shocked the Tudor court by marrying Thomas Seymour a few weeks after the king's death on January 28, 1547. Sadly, she would not outlive the king by many years; on September 7, 1548, she would die in childbirth.

I admired the elegant Katherine Parr,
thought her beauty worth polishing each facet
of that jade-encrusted cross she wore at mass,
and certainly worth creating things spectacular—
those spirals of rubies, clusters of rosettes
that shone in her auburn hair like polished glass.

So I grew smug, so easily believing
eternity was embedded in a wire twist,
that seams, once soldered, would hold at vital joints.
But fibers, pounded thin, can be deceiving;
since, under pressure, few metals can resist
bending and breaking at their weakest points.

For my world collapsed at milady's passing—
Why, I asked angrily, *are the finest gems
so easily loosened, so easily lost?*
And so I mourned, my misery outlasting
the soulful ritual of her requiem,
as I let bitterness claim its dreadful cost.

Wiser now, I take refuge in reflection,
grateful when memories awaken the past—
for grief begs introspection, spurs us to pray—
and mine is a sorrow eased by recollection
of a goodness and beauty rarely surpassed.
I now know joy can be salvaged, just the way

pearls can be restrung and evenly spread,
radiance coiled around a reknotted thread.

ELIZABETH TUDOR ON HER SISTER'S CORONATION, 1553

After the death of Edward VI, Mary Tudor, half-sister of Elizabeth I, is crowned Queen of England, making Elizabeth next-in-line to the throne.

Half-hidden under a silver-threaded canopy,
my sister preceded me on that triumphal walk
from Whitehall Palace to the portal of Westminster.
And if I was surprised by the streets hung with banners,
carpeted with just-picked flowers, lined with cheering crowds
welling with fervor at this sight of their sovereign,
remember I was raised in rural obscurity
so I rejoiced in the pageantry of crimson-clad lords,
the extravagance of conduits flowing with claret,
the fragrance of tapers perfuming a southern wind—
until we stepped into the vastness of Westminster
where Mary was glorified, deemed divine and apart
as she accepted bracelets of gold,
Sceptre, Orb and Spurs,
before kneeling for that ancient, last anointing.
Then I shivered and grew cold with understanding—
for my simple coronet proclaimed me a princess,
but a step away from that diamond-encrusted crown.

THE LIFE OF ELIZABETH II IN NUMBERS

Like her namesake, Elizabeth I, Elizabeth II has had a long and successful reign.

She has reigned almost four times as long as her father
but still not as long as Queen Victoria,
her great great grandmother who died at eighty-one.

For better or worse, every year for eighty days
she is four years younger than the Duke of Edinburgh,
her husband of sixty-eight years, over half her life.

On the practical side, she is the only Brit
who can drive without a license or registration,
travel out of the country without a passport,

and claim ownership of eighty-eight cygnets,
those young swans in residence on the River Thames.
Each year she hosts more than fifty thousand people

at banquets and teas in Buckingham Palace,
not to mention launching the first royal website,
or being the first British princess in wartime

to save ration coupons for her wedding dress—
before introducing the breed dorgi (not corgi)
to a world needing royals with a common touch.

Bibliography

Brown, Tina. *The Diana Chronicles*. Broadway Books, 2008.

Frazer, Antonia. *The Wives of Henry VIII*. Alfred A. Knopf, 1992.

Luke, Mary M. *A Crown for Elizabeth*. Coward McCann, Inc., 1970.

Marshall, Rosalind K. *Mary of Guise*. Collins, 1977.

Swain, Margaret. *The Needlework of Mary, Queen of Scots*. Reinhold Co., 1973.

Long fascinated by the queens of sixteenth century Britain, Carol Milkuhn has explored this interest through both prose and poetry. Her first novel, *A Tapestry of Queens*, grew out of a prize-winning poem, "Anne Boleyn's Dressmaker." Other of her prize-winning poems have appeared in *The Copperfield Review, Vermont Literary Review, The Mountain Troubadour*, and online at *WinningWriters.com.* and *Literal Latte.com.* A retired English teacher, Carol holds a Masters degree from the University of Michigan and has studied at the University of Edinburgh in Scotland. She lives and writes in Vermont.

www.ingramcontent.com/pod-product-compliance
Lightning Source LLC
LaVergne TN
LVHW041330080426
835513LV00008B/659